4 STEPS
TO NOT ALLOWING THE
PANDEMIC
TO AFFECT YOUR
HOME

RET. LTC Consuelo Castillo Kickbusch
&
Roy Juarez, Jr.

4 Steps to Not Allowing the Pandemic to Affect your Home
Copyright © 2020 by IMPACTtruth, Inc.
& Educational Achievement Services, Inc.

All rights reserved. This book or any portion thereof
may not be reproduced or used in any manner whatsoever
without the express written permission of the publisher
except for the use of brief quotations in a book review.

United States of America

1st Edition, 2020

ISBN 978-1-7325507-3-5

IMPACT Publishing, Inc.
P.O. Box 27311
San Antonio, TX 78251

www.IMPACTmemoirs.com
www.EASLeadership.com

Dedication

This book is dedicated to all the unsung heroes and sheroes who are on the front lines risking their lives to save a wounded world.

To all medical field professionals, migrant workers, and to our men and women in blue, we are forever grateful. We will keep you and your families in our prayers.

To the educators and administrators who are working so hard to keep our children learning, thank you for not giving up on our most important treasures.

To parents and guardians, while it is a complicated time we are living in, you are the thread that is holding this nation together. This book is written as a tool to help you stay strong and strengthen your family.

To everyone I've mentioned and to the people I haven't, never give up.

Table of Contents

ACKNOWLEDGMENTS I

FOREWORD VII

INTRODUCTION IX

STEP 1 - STAY HUMAN 1

STEP 2 - IT'S GOING TO BE OKAY 23

STEP 3 - MINIMIZE STRESS, MAXIMIZE JOY 55

STEP 4 - EDUCATE & EMPOWER 89

FINAL THOUGHTS 113

OTHER BOOKS BY THESE AUTHORS. 115

ABOUT THE AUTHORS 119

Acknowledgments

To the Pandemic, we know what you did, and we will never forget. However, you will not write our last chapter. To your credit, you slowed us down, allowing us time to reflect on what is most important. You gave us a chance to love deeper, which brought us closer together and strengthened our family, community, and our faith in humanity.

Our Quarantine Bunkmates:

Gregory A. Williams, the person who made us pause, sit down, and eat at the table like a family. You fed us amazing meals on a budget and frankly you are the reason why we now must get a gym membership once this pandemic is over. We are so grateful. We can't wait for you to open up your restaurant. Count us in as your first paying customers. — Roy and Consuelo

Ray C. Reynosa AKA Pup, your title is Executive Assistant but, for this project, you really served as the IT-guy, personal shopper, editor, light technician, ... the list goes on.

I will admit you drove me crazy, but I also realize I drove you crazy as well. You made me laugh, helped me with anything I needed, and most of all, you made it possible for me to focus on this book. Thank you for everything, Pup. I love you! — Consuelo

You are an amazing baby brother, and I am so proud of you! Your compassion for others, creativity, and heart of gold will take you far. Thank you for all your insight and willingness to wash and fold my clothes so I could focus on this book. I love you. - Your brother, Roy

Delilah and Dolores Kickbusch, my twin daughters, who are among my favorite children. You both stepped up to do the many chores that as young children got you grounded enough... Thank you! —- Mom (Consuelo)

You two rock! Thank you for always making room for me in your family and life. I will always love you two with all my heart, no matter what!!! — Roy

To Our Families:

Consuelo: David Allen Kickbusch, Kenitha Calisa White, Iliana Perez, Alicia Carmelina Evans, Sean Sarles, Dorian Castillo Sarles, Aria Sarles, Consuelo Martin, Daniel Martin, Delilah Kickbusch and Dolores Kickbusch. Cynthia Rocha, Robert Rocha, Antonio Daniel Rocha and Paloma Catalina Rocha **Pets:** Choco, Cholula, and Cheto who is now famous thanks to this book. I may have left out a hamster or two. Is Cinnamon still alive?

Roy: To my family, my love for you is beyond words. You are the reason I do what I do and never give up. I couldn't survive this world without you all. Thank you for putting up with my crazy ideas and work as an activist. I wouldn't trade any of you for anything. I am truly blessed!

Our Support Team:

Reggie Nerio and Baby Nova, thank you for finding a way to work while caring for a teething toddler, our hats are off to you. Your gift of editing makes us look like we at least have half a brain! — Roy and Consuelo

Nathan Hassall, our editor-in-chief and prolific re-writer of rough content. Really, thank you, our friend. We know this Pandemic has kept you in England for longer than you anticipated so you could care for your father. We will forever be grateful that you took the time to help us. Also, thank you for providing us with a discount while we are jobless; we promise to make it up to you. Just you wait for this book to become a bestseller! — Roy and Consuelo

Remmy Castillo, my favorite nephew (wink wink), I want to give you a huge thank you for sharing your million-dollar talents and heart. I know you would do anything for your favorite Tia (Auntie). — Consuelo

It has been an honor getting to you know. You are brilliant! — Roy

Dr. Hendershott and Dardi Hendershott, you are both too kind. Thank you for your friendship and taking the chance to help your crazy friends for life. Dardi, you are the beautiful one, just don't tell Joe! - Roy and Consuelo

Last but not least

To you, the reader, the courageous ones, we may not know you, but our spirits are connected through this unparalleled time. May our words inspire, motivate, and empower you to write a wonderful ending to this chapter in your family's life and not allow the pandemic to affect your home.

Thank you for allowing us into your life, we hope you find value in our book.

Foreword

In this life, none of us are immune to adversity. When we face these hardships, we tend to look for the helpers... Someone, anyone who will understand how we feel and provide a ray of hope toward better days.

Roy and Consuelo have both faced adversities in their lives, but instead of being rendered helpless by them, they have used them as a catalyst toward directing others on a path toward wholeness, empowerment, and healing.

Through this same lens, Roy and Consuelo have authored the book *4 Steps to Not Allowing the Pandemic to Affect Your HOME* in response to this present adversity that has all of us looking for helpers.

Roy and Consuelo share from the heart, strategies that will encourage and empower people with actionable steps that can be practiced daily to create cohesive environments where we can thrive together through this pandemic with purpose, joy, and hope.

Dr. Joe & Dardi Hendershott
Co-Founders, Hope 4 The Wounded
Authors, *Supporting the Wounded Educator: A Trauma-Sensitive Approach to Self-Care*
7 Ways to Transform the Lives of Wounded Students
Reaching the Wounded Student
www.hope4thewounded.org

Introduction

Here we are, six of us—three different families, plus one chihuahua named Cheeto (Cheto, if you're bilingual)—quarantined in a 1,500 square foot home in Las Vegas. Yes, some of us really do live here. No, not all of us spend all our time gambling in the casinos.

This is a household of giving and accepting. Our goal is to be as selfless with each other as possible. We are sharing our food, fears, laughs, and faith. Most importantly, we are sharing our love.

Most of our conversation has centered on how we are feeling, our concern for our families, but most importantly, trying to approach this pandemic with a leveled head.

We started to question; What would our elders have done in this situation? Since they were so resilient, and much of our success is attributed to them. We are actively learning from the past to inform our future decision making.

In these pages, you will discover Roy's reflections and thoughts on dealing with a global pandemic, through his lens of being a homeless youth before maturing into the entrepreneur and activist he is today.

You will also discover a part of Consuelo's story, a daughter of immigrants, an Army veteran, social activist, and entrepreneur, as she discusses how to strengthen your home during this pandemic through the lens of her immigrant parents and lifelong professional careers.

We both agree that the moral of our stories are fundamentally about strengthening the HOME. Each of the letters from HOME comprise the sections of this book.

However, the pages below will explore a rollercoaster of emotions, including anxiety, hope, fear, anger, and gratitude, that are pushing us to make various choices as to what becomes our truths.

May this book serve as inspiration and hope for our friends and families. May it bless you and empower you to take action so that no family stops making a home for themselves.

With Ultimate Dignity,

~ Roy and Consuelo

*"It's not how big the house is,
it's how happy the home is."*

- Unknown

H.O.M.E.

STEP 1 - *Stay Human*

Dealing with the Unexpected
~ From the lens of Roy

As the morning approached, the sun peeked through the vertical, off-white Venetian blinds, creating slabs of rectangular light throughout the room. One of the rectangles ran perfectly across my eyes causing me to squint. Before the inevitable headache of an early-morning wake-up, I quickly rolled over on the couch. I wasn't ready for the day.

This was all the cruder as I was taken out of a dream I was enjoying. I was at a family gathering back home in San Antonio. My nieces had surrounded me, asking me to play cards with them. They all hugged me, and I felt the warm buzz of love from their touch. The sweet scent of maple bacon wafted from the kitchen. My mom asked me if I was hungry. My mouth dripped with anticipation.

That dream felt so real, so human, so *normal*. But here I was, being serenaded by the soft snores of my baby (but adult) brother Ray on my left and my roommate Greg, who was traveling with me, on my right. I failed to get back to sleep, moved onto my back, opened my eyes, and stared at the ceiling. I couldn't help but chuckle to myself. I wondered, *Is this my new reality?*

I grew up as a homeless teenager due to domestic violence, and while that was many, many years ago, it didn't take long for those same emotions and fears I had as a teen to creep back in.

I knew I wasn't the only one worried. The COVID-19 (a coronavirus disease) pandemic has been the only thing people had been talking about for weeks. I had read articles, Facebook posts, and watched so many news clips about the pandemic, and it was difficult to not allow fear to settle in. Perhaps my overindulgence in keeping up to date with it all via the news was detrimental to my mental health, but I found it difficult to look away. This gripped the world, and it gripped me too.

COVID-19 started in a wild animal, meat, and fish market in Wuhan, China in November 2019. It took some time for it to spread, and it wasn't until January that our media really started taking notice of it.

The infection—which spreads easily through droplets (from touching the mouth or nose, coughing, or sneezing) and gets into our bodies via our mucus membranes (through the nose, eyes, or mouth)—ranges in its severity from person-to-person.

Some who are infected are asymptomatic, others have mild symptoms like a week-long dry cough and elevated temperature, others suffer from high fevers, shortness of breath, and other respiratory difficulties, and in the worst-case scenarios, some suffer from severe pneumonia (requiring respiratory assistance from medical ventilators), organ failure, and even death.

At the onset of the pandemic, there was so much uncertainty and contradicting messages reported on mainstream media I had no idea who or what to believe. I'm sure many of you felt the same.

Ultimately, fear made its way into my heart and mind, as I was scared not only for myself, but for my family, friends, employees, and the global community. I didn't want anyone close to me to get sick, and I was left with no work and my employees' livelihoods in my hands.

There was no more disputing that the pandemic was affecting everyone. After all, my friend Reagan in Italy was posting about it. My friend/our editor Nathan was caring for his ill father in England, who had two hospital visits as the result of the virus.

My best friend Marco, who owns several boutique hotels in Brazil, shared with me that everyone was canceling their reservations, and I was quarantined with five other people in my mentor's condo, sleeping on her couch.

As the springs of the couch pressed deep into my back, the homeless little boy inside of me came back to life. I wondered; *Would I be homeless again?*

For a brief second, I entertained that thought, but then I looked over and saw Ray, sleeping next to me peacefully. Twenty-four years ago, he was lying next to me as a two-year-old homeless child, but today, with hard work, faith, and perseverance, he is a college graduate and an exceptional young man who will go on to achieve beyond what I ever thought was possible for our family all those years ago.

Looking at Ray restored hope in me. If we could make it on the streets, we can make it through this. A huge grin stretched across my face. I know where I came from and how to overcome hardship. I didn't come this far by allowing fear to hold me back; I made it this far by finding solutions to my problems and never giving up.

What were some of the tools that brought me through the hard times of my youth? The times that I had no idea where I was going to sleep or find my next meal.

During those turbulent times of my youth, I quickly learned the only thing that I was able to control was how I perceived situations. So, I started to search for joy, happy memories, or anything that would bring me positivity despite the hardships of my current reality.

For many years, I chose the negative path. I began drinking heavily to self-medicate and could not maintain a job because I was too hungover to go to work. I knew something had to change, and I realized I had the choice of looking at life through either a negative lens or a positive lens.

I thought, *Life sucks, no one loves me, and I can't trust anyone.* I wanted to blame someone or something for why life would never get better for me. In the end, that negative mindset just complicated my life, I developed bad habits, and I could never seem to get ahead.

It wasn't until I shifted towards a positive outlook that things began to change. I trained myself to see things not as a setback, but as a blessing.

For example, when I was moving from home to home and living out of a bag, I had dealt with so much stress — I didn't know how to manage it effectively. On the other hand, having lived with so many different people, I quickly learned "interpersonal communication." I had become so creative with turning my negatives into positives that I started to discover the gifts my "setbacks" really gave me. My life began to change.

Life isn't easy, especially during a pandemic. However, we can't lose sight of the joy, the good times, or the hidden lessons that this situation can teach us. If we look closely, we will find them, even if we find them in the memories of those we have lost or been separated from.

There are true stories out there of heroes and heroines. Our healthcare workers are risking their lives and health to save others. People are working in shops, warehouses, delivery service industries, and migrant workers are still out picking crops to ensure people can get food. There are public transportation workers ensuring our healthcare and other vital workers are able to get to work. There are hospital cleaners, ensuring the conditions of the hospital are sanitary and help limit the spread of the virus. Citizens are delivering food and medication to those who are at-risk.

In the United Kingdom, in an attempt to get citizens to volunteer to help the NHS (National Health Service), their government sent out an appeal for volunteers, and they hoped to get 250,000 signing up in three days. However, in just 24 hours, they surpassed that number. At the time of writing this, they exceeded just over half a million volunteers. Truly amazing.

If this pandemic has taught me anything, it reminds me of how fragile life really is. This *ah-ha* moment was solidified when I received a text message in my family group chat. The news came from my sister, "I may be infected. I will keep everyone updated. I'm in tears right now. Staying positive, but I'm still scared." A few hours later, a text from my dad came in that read, "This is very difficult to do, but I'm sure you will all understand, please keep your distance. As you all know, me and mom will likely not survive if the virus gets to us."

Little did I know, days later, I would receive the worst of news.

My mother sent a message to our family chat that read, "My family, it saddens me to say that I am officially under self-quarantine, effective today for the next 14 days. It's a safety precaution. I feel fine and in good spirits, just pray for us. My co-worker got sick and just tested positive for the virus."

I have visited my mother many times at her job and she works in a small, confined room with six other people. My siblings and I knew the severity of the text.

My little sister Danielle replied, "This officially sucks! I don't know what I would do if I lost you." I couldn't agree with her more. I would be devastated and unable to function for months if I lost my mother.

These two text messages sent chills down my spine that I can't put into words adequately. However, as I learned from previous experiences, I have a choice. I can stay stuck in that moment of fear and despair, or I can find joy and hope, and push forward for my family and loved ones.

We will all face adversity, but this is one of those times that all of mankind faces it together. While this pandemic has taken some of our jobs, freedom, and loved ones, what we must never allow it to take is our humanity.

The Elder Story
~ From the lens of Consuelo

*I **was raised*** by a pastor father and a missionary mother who, through the example they set to others, had unwavering faith. Since they are no longer by my side, I imagine how they would face this pandemic the same way they lived their lives each day. They would rise with the sun, get out of bed, and put their knees to the floor. There, at the foot of their bed, they would start their day with grateful words, prayers for others, and a humble request to stay strong for their family even though little food was available and there wasn't much work going around. This would heal their souls even though they knew they would have to face another difficult day.

My dad, the jokester and endless optimist, would wake up my siblings and me by asking, "Do y'all want papas con huevos (potatoes with eggs) or huevos con papas (eggs with potatoes)?" As a kid, hungry and still sleepy, I would look over to one of my siblings, puzzled, and slowly realize he was pulling our leg. A que mi Papi (oh my dad) — the ultimate positive person.

I started with this story because of my father's teachings. (I used the word 'teaching' although he would argue that he didn't ever teach, he in fact 'preached and practiced'.) Since the start of the quarantine, I have prayed and then stepped into the living room to ask myself, *What will I feed my family today?* Knowing I had to make do with what was in my cupboards.

It used to be so easy to say, "I will be right back" and head to the store when food was low, but we can't do this at the moment. Especially those of us who are over 65 years old.

To think, going to the grocery store could become a death sentence. I ask myself, *is this our new norm?* How will our lives change and will we become a better world more in tune with each other, more willing to help each other, and stress less over the petty things that we used to put so much emphasis on like having to wait to get our nails done or stand in line at the checkout in a grocery store?

In my father's case, he would have to struggle and wonder how he was going to get through the day when he was poor, had ten kids, a wife that struggled with mental illness, and an elderly father-in-law.

Just one of these truths can get the best of you, and every day for most of my life, this was my reality. It is likely that you, too, will go down your mental list at some point and wonder what else can happen or go wrong. You may already be at the point of anger, fear, or resentment. It takes conscious self-awareness and courageous leadership to rise above the noise, whether it is in your head or the damn washer that endlessly whirs and whirs.

My dad was my hero. As a young man, he found himself traveling wherever work was to be found, which brought him to the United States, the Land of Opportunity. As he would say in his Spanish accent, "Amereeka."

He spent a large part of his life working in the coal mines around Texas, places like Goliath and Corsicana. Then he moved onto the steel mills of Illinois, and eventually, as time passed and his health deteriorated, he accepted any day laborer work that came his way.

My poor Mami (Mother) was always moving, cooking, and finding means to hold the family together. She did this and more, all while coping with the burden of chronic depression — a term we didn't learn about until much later in life. It must have been too much for her at times. Papi, although he suffered severe burns, and even lost several of his fingers to provide his children a chance at a better life, one thing was constant: he was always hopeful and laughed often.

He constantly tried to make my mom laugh, and while it was annoying to my mother, for she was the worrier, we would catch her turning around to smile or walking away, chuckling.

My father accepted God and became a devout Christian, eventually becoming a pastor and dedicating his life to helping others until his passing at the age of 83. I miss my dad dearly.

My mother lived with me upon my father's passing and the good news is that since she became my military dependent she got help for her mental illness. Imagine waiting until you are sixty to finally get help. Her words upon taking the correct medicine were, "So this is what it feels to be a normal person Hija (daughter)?" I miss her strength and singing those gospel songs that I now have on tape sustain me. She was a wounded and complex woman, and still my heroine.

This Too Shall Pass

Healing is not an end to our pain or suffering. Just like this pandemic, we shall suffer job loss, tension at home, and anxiety, and dark thoughts will cross our minds. I remember telling my family all of my work had been canceled.

The news reports about how soon we could begin to take our lives back kept getting worse and worse, but I wasn't going to sit around and do nothing. I asked my family to help me help ourselves. We had to figure out what we could do differently, and although we were about to take on a new reality, a passage I've always held on to came to mind: *This too shall pass.*

It's admirable to see your family step up and get things done. Echoing Roy's sentiment, you can do something positive and let the folks who surround you know you love them. Perhaps this pandemic has brought us closer, taught us to be grateful for each other, and pushed us to be creative with what we have available. Have you noticed board games are now popular again? They might even be cooler than video games, and young people might fall in love with real-world socializing again (okay, maybe I'm being *too* hopeful).

I want you to pause for a moment. Take a deep breath and center yourself. Now ask yourself, *Am I the only one in this situation?* By recognizing how much of the world is in the same position, we know we are not alone. So, instead of internalizing or taking the apathetic approach, we can make the choice to become empathetic and compassionate, which gives us the ability to heal our souls.

We must make sure that we are *Being Human* and not just being *Human Beings*. What makes us human is our ability to feel and act with love and kindness. There is a Couture Designer who is now making masks for health workers; an ICU Nurse that is putting family members on Facetime so they can connect emotionally or, in the worst-case scenario, say goodbye; there is an elderly lady who is being serenaded by her neighbor's children, reminding her she is not alone.

Chris Cuomo, the CNN anchor and now at home with COVID-19, said the following so beautifully, "Americans, we can Amer I Can." All over the world, we all *can* do something. Look into your heart, and if nothing else, say a prayer for hope and healing.

This too shall pass.

4 STEPS TO NOT ALLOWING THE PANDEMIC TO AFFECT YOUR HOME

Reflective questions:

1) What lessons have you learned from the past that can be applied now?

2) Who has a significant place in your heart, and have you called them? Take action now.

3) What random act of kindness can you offer even while at home? Perhaps you could make this an activity for the whole family.

4) What has the pandemic taught you thus far?

5) While in quarantine, what little things have brought you joy?

4 STEPS TO NOT ALLOWING THE PANDEMIC TO AFFECT YOUR HOME

H.O.M.E.

STEP 2 - *It's Going to be Okay*

El Rincón Del Diablo
~ *From the lens of Consuelo*

When you grow up with seven brothers and two tougher sisters, you learn quickly to 'suck it up 'and be strong. Add to that, being raised in a tough Barrio (hood) with a name like El Rincón Del Diablo (The Devil's Den), you understand you need to stay stoic, learn the ways of the streets, and know when to keep your mouth shut.

Still, I am a child pretending to be tough on the outside but a little girl yearning for love and nurturing on the inside. I saw the outcomes of poverty, gangs, drugs, and violence.

Now, with the pandemic, many are saying the same outcomes will begin to manifest or intensify. We can change history and end this pandemic on many fronts, not just medically but emotionally, psychologically, and physically. We now can choose to become a better family, community, country, and world.

I am hopeful that we, as a society, will overcome these obstacles just as my community did even in a tough neighborhood like ours. That we can still care genuinely for each other and know we have each other's back.

In the tribal nature I was raised in we shared in the good times, and we shared in the bad times.

For example, I recall whenever my mother would cook a bit too much of something. It became a ritual to send the many kids out to share the food with our neighbors. Forget Grubhub! Just let the Castillo tribe do the delivery. Not long after this act of kindness, hot meals would travel back to our family. What goes around comes around.

Moving South

The year was 1947, and desperation hit. My parents knew the inevitable had come; they needed to move their family in search of work again.

At the time, they had four young boys, no transportation, but a vision that, through hope, support from others, and tons of courage laced with faith, it was going to be okay.

Do you sometimes wonder when you hear of such stories, *How were they able to find success in the end?* Vision is not just a metaphor; it is a practice that all of us possess, and with it comes courage, faith, and guts to act upon it.

My parents were uprooted again in 1953. They took a long train ride from Sterling, Illinois to Laredo, Texas, a total of 1,311 miles. Once they got off, they wondered, *What now?*

With an aging and ill father, a mother who still struggled with mental illness, they experienced the surprise that another child was on the way. Yes, that child was me.

Some may deem them irresponsible for bringing another child into the world, but my parents loved each other, and in the end, it was their decision. I have chosen not to judge, but to learn from their good and not-so-good choices.

During the Pandemic, we'll probably see a spike in birth rates, after all, what are you supposed to do with all this time?!

Life is indeed cyclical: some will be born, and some will leave us. I grew up with these parents who never complained, always laughed —even at themselves—and taught us to laugh at ourselves.

Once again, they moved but remained in Laredo, where El Rincon Del Diablo would become my home.

Sixty-seven years after this, they had over 100 descendants, most of them jokesters.

Among the king of all jokesters is Benny, my 82-year-old brother. Several days ago, he sent an email asking, "how was I doing?"

I replied (jokingly because I couldn't help myself), How wonderful it must be to be at home to do all the laundry, cook, clean, wash the dishes, give foot massages, mow the lawn, take the dogs for a walk, and much more... all to help his wife out.

He completely ignored the question in my email and simply wrote, the only noticeable things he saw were the animals in his rural community were not wearing masks!

We must be careful about what we envision and the steps we take to reach our end goal. Like my parents, who overcame their challenging move, we all want to come out of our hardships as better people, cognizant of each other's journey with empathy and love for all.

Shifting False Beliefs into Truths

Refuge comes not just from where we look, but by asking ourselves where we did not look.

Among my treasured friends are Dr. Joe Hendershott and his wife, Mrs. Dardi Hendershott, highly respected authors and thought leaders on the topic of wounded students and wounded educators.

Their books, *Reaching the Wounded Student* and *Seven Ways to Transform the Lives of Wounded Students* are filled with a wealth of knowledge so appropriate for us to know during this pandemic.

Recently they finished a book entitled *Supporting the Wounded Educator: A Trauma-Sensitive Approach to Self-Care*. Among my "a-ha" moments from their work, I learned the difference between being "at-risk" and being "wounded," and how being wounded can conjure up "false beliefs" within ourselves.

Here is how they define the difference between the two, "We all can be at-risk of something like catching a cold or not finishing high school; however, being wounded stems from adverse past experiences that now are surfacing by other triggers in our life".

How many people will now be wounded because of the pandemic? How many more will suffer from PTSD (Post Traumatic Stress Disorder)? More than ever, we need to be more informed and read about how we can be more supportive of our wounded neighbors.

As to false beliefs, Joe and Dardi share the story about their young, adopted daughter who said to Joe, "Nobody loves me" in response to frustration over a difficult situation.

He responded, "I love you, and your mother loves you." She then adjusted her belief and said, "You love me, and Mother loves me, but no one else loves me." This was yet another opportunity to pour truth into her false beliefs by naming others who also love her: Teachers, friends, relatives, ...

How beautiful that a young child who was responding through the lens of her wounds was given a new perspective, which in turn shifted her "false beliefs" into "truths" that she was loved and not alone.

I could go on and on about how much their work has touched my spirit and helped me, but I truly believe it would be better if you heard it from them.

I highly recommend their work to you because, during times such as this, our children, and perhaps even you, may be triggered by wounds and succumb to false beliefs and feelings of hopelessness.

In such a short time, I have had many False Beliefs. I have come a long way from being a dysfunctional person full of anger and resentment. However, with the pandemic, I experienced deja vu, and I had to shift away from thinking that I was the only one working hard in my team because my employees were not connecting with me via phone or email. I had to become more aware of our generational differences.

The Walking ATM

This pandemic, despite the difficulties it's caused me and everyone else around the globe, has done something marvelous. It has taught us that now more than ever, we are intergenerationally dependent, and it's stretching all of us to operate differently. If anything, we are growing to understand each other more, and the barrier between the generations is thinning.

The merging of these two generations, boomers, and millennials, will serve as a steep learning curve, and it is up to members of both generations to be open-minded and understanding.

These young ones are light years ahead of us when it comes to technology, but they need our wisdom, support, and (perhaps most critically!) our money. After all, we are just a walking ATM.

Unknown to me, my team was looking for other opportunities using technology; they were filling out paperwork for economic relief, reaching out to past clients, and working on putting our Family Leadership Institute curriculum online.

When I learned of their efforts, I felt terrible and reminded myself to stay on my path, get out of the weeds, and focus on my talents. I thought to myself, *Do you not trust your team? Do you not remember when in other times they rose above and exceeded your expectations?*

Now more than ever I had to practice courageous leadership, because micromanaging and endless meetings that go nowhere can be replaced by giving folks the space to be creative and push innovative and fresh ideas front and center.

There are many technological tools you can use to see who is really connected and being productive. Don't forget you can always have a Virtual Employee of the Month or a Happy Hour on Friday via Zoom — and don't forget to invite us!

This brings me to the youngest member of my team, who I will discuss later in the book, because it's a story of education and empowerment.

Coffee and Confessions
~ *From the lens of Roy*

As I was quietly folding my blankets, trying not to wake anyone else, I noticed my mentor, who is like my mother, peeking around the corner of the hall that led to her room. I could tell she had just woken up. Her hands were clasped, as though in prayer, and her hair was pulled back.

"Are you awake?" She asked in a whisper.

"No, I'm sleepwalking." I laughed.

"Well then." She rolled her eyes with a smile. "Would you like some coffee to help wake you up?"

I smiled and replied, "Yes, please!"

She walked into the kitchen as I continued putting my bed away. When I was done, I tiptoed towards the kitchen, stepping over Greg, who was sleeping on the floor. As I entered the kitchen, my mentor handed me a cup of coffee.

"Come on, let's drink this on the balcony to get some sun," she suggested as she picked up her cup. We walked back down the hallway, through her room, and she opened the door to the back balcony.

As I stepped through the threshold crisp, cold air hit my face. The temperature was cool enough to wake me up and enjoy the hot coffee, but not too cold that I needed to turn back around.

As soon as I went to sit on the steel patio chair, I jumped up faster than I had sat down. Burr. My mentor sat without even flinching — she's always been tougher than me! We both let out a jovial howl, but quickly shushed each other and chuckled because we didn't want to wake the others.

Staring off into the distance, watching the beautiful city of Las Vegas wake up, I said, "Not that many cars as usual, huh?"

"No, not at all," she replied.

I looked over towards her as she sipped her coffee. I smiled. "Thank you for having all of us here during these times."

"You don't have to thank me. You are my son. My toilet paper is your toilet paper and no need to recycle please." she replied.
We both laughed and I wrapped my hands tighter around my warm coffee mug.

"This morning I had the most interesting experience," I began. "I woke and just laid there in my thoughts. For a second, I was 14 again, homeless and afraid."

She leaned in towards me.

"I think it was just the fear of losing all my work and trying to figure out how I'm going to keep my company alive. I think that fear triggered me and reminded me of the fears of my youth."

"Ay Mijo (my son)," she responded. "You are not that 14-year-old anymore."

"I know ma'am." I glanced at my shoes, then back at her.
"Plus, you have me, and you're a college graduate. Look how far you have come."

"That's true." I took in a breath. "You want to know something?"

"Ay, Dios Mio (oh my God), is it confession time?" She chuckled. I knew she was trying to lift my spirits.

"No, no, it's nothing like that." I paused and took another gulp of my coffee, edging closer to the thick sludge at the bottom of the mug. "I was lying there feeling scared earlier, but when I looked over and saw

Baby Ray, he gave me hope. I realized how far we had come when I considered my baby brother is a man."

She nodded. "What we need is hope, but we can't just sit here and hope, we have to put hope into action."

"I agree, ma'am. In my company, we were trying to figure out a way to give back, so we created "Reading with Reggie." Every Tuesday and Thursday, my Operations Manager goes on Facebook Live and reads to children. Since we are all in quarantine, we figured by having her read, it would be great to give the parents a break." I sat there for a second, proud to share my idea.

"Oh, that's so great!" She took a deep inhale and exhaled with a grin. "At EAS (Educational Achievement Services) we've been making food baskets for some of the families we work with. We're doing as much as we can Hijo (son).."

"That's what we are doing, too!" I shifted in the uncomfortable chair.

"We all have to do our part and use whatever talent we have to help each other. I mean, look at us, we're sharing our resources to help it stretch.

It reminds me of when I was younger, and one of the neighborhood kids came over for dinner, or when my parents took in another family to help. My mom would say, 'I'll add a little more water to the beans.' It was never a question if it was enough; we just made it work."

"So, are we having bean soup for breakfast?" I joked.

"I don't know, what are you cooking for us?"

We both laughed.

"I'll be right back, let me go check on everyone," I said as I got up from my chair. I walked back through the bedroom, down the hall, and into the living area. Everyone was up and moving. Greg was in the kitchen, making everyone breakfast. Baby Ray was putting away their sleeping areas while the twins, my mentor's daughters, were setting the table for the meal.

"Well, Good morning everyone!" I said. Each one greeted me back, and all seemed in high spirits. I stood there for a second and watched each person fulfill a role. I grinned and thought to myself, *we are going to make it through this because we're all pitching in.*

The Rollercoaster Begins

The next few days, every morning was the same. Everyone got up, went to their station, and started acting out their roles. However, as each day passed, I noticed there was a little less joy. I think everyone's use of their gifts became more of a job, which was taking the wind out of people's sails.

When the "Safer at Home" emergency order came, it didn't sink in how difficult it would prove to be. The first day of being quarantined was easy. I think we all thought, *It's just another day.*

By the third day, the reality of the situation was starting to set in for everyone. There were only so many rooms you could go into, only so many hours you could sit and watch TV, and the same board game began to lose its excitement.

It might have been a little harder on Greg, Ray, and me because we weren't in our own space. We were in someone else's space, and even though my mentor is like our mother, it still wasn't our home.

It's similar to the feeling of finally moving out of your parent's house; you never really want to go back because you have experienced what it's like living on your own, but you still don't want your mom to turn your bedroom into a home gym.

By the end of the fourth day, I think we all started to climb the walls, and the feeling of being cooped up was affecting everyone differently.

The twins sat in their bedroom most of the time, Ray wanted to go hiking or sit outside alone, and Greg spent most of his time cooking and cleaning the kitchen over and over again, not to mention slamming the cabinet doors during our intense brainstorming sessions. (wink wink) It's probably the cleanest and most organized place in all of North America.

Mrs. Kickbusch and I tried to get lost in our work. We were reaching out to colleagues, creating new workshops, and jumping on zoom calls — the list goes on.

I am not sure if it was the mounting stress of trying to figure out how to keep my own company alive, being cooped up, or losing all my work, but I felt like I needed to get out. I decided I was going to head back home to Los Angeles. Equipped with disinfectant wipes and hand sanitizer, I was ready to make the 4-hour drive home.

Greg and I said our goodbyes to my mentor, the twins, and Ray. Ray wasn't coming with us because he was doing an internship with Mrs. Kickbusch.

Greg insisted on driving, so I relaxed in the passenger seat. As we got on I-15 south for Los Angeles, I brought up my emails to review them. I opened an email from our apartment complex, stating we had a resident who tested positive for COVID 19. I immediately turned over to look at Greg. "Someone in our apartment complex just tested positive."

"Oh no..." Greg broke his view from the road and looked over at me with his eyes wide open. "What do you want to do?"

Whether it was fear or wisdom, I said, "I can't get sick." I knew if I got sick, I wouldn't be able to work and pay my employees. I took a screenshot of the email and texted it to my mentor and little brother. In just a few short minutes, my mentor was calling me. In a panic, she said, "Come back! It's not worth it. We would feel so much better if you just come back here with us."

I felt stuck. I knew it would be hard to stay quarantined somewhere other than my apartment, but I didn't want to go home because I was scared of getting sick.

I think my mentor could sense my stress. "I noticed the hotel next door dropped its rates to $39 a night. If you need space, you can go there for a few nights. I think they even have a kitchen! However, Greg stays with us, let him know he can slam all the doors he wants." she explained.

The idea didn't sound too bad, (not about Greg but about the hotel) because I knew it would help me focus on work and I wouldn't have to worry about getting sick. At that rate, I could stay a full week and it would still be affordable. Although I would have to tap into my savings, if Greg was willing to stay, we could split the cost.

The next thing I knew, we had turned the car around and headed back to Las Vegas. I know this might sound crazy, going to Vegas during the pandemic, but it wasn't like that. We weren't on vacation.

The truth is, it's eerie to see the strip so dead and cops on every corner. It felt like a movie; it was either the end of the world or a zombie apocalypse.

Every casino was closed, and the only people who were roaming the streets were people filming how empty the Las Vegas strip was—a city that usually hosted over 42 million visitors a year—the police, and the homeless.

More Than Four Walls

The word 'homeless 'is interesting to me because many people don't really put thought to it. They hear the word 'homeless 'and automatically think about a person sleeping on the street. While in fact, there are many other levels.

Webster's definition of homeless is *having no home or permanent place of residence*.

One level is situational or transitional homelessness, when a person or family is forced into homelessness due to a life-altering event such as a death, job loss, domestic violence, medical emergency, or a natural disaster.

Even with the ban on evictions throughout the country, it is going to be hard for families to recover from lost wages. The aftermath of this pandemic is just as worrying as it is to be in the throes of it. The idea that over 6.6 million people and counting are applying for unemployment is devastating.

This doesn't mean all families or individuals will be out on the streets. Oftentimes, during situational or transitional homelessness, individuals or families may bounce from hotel to hotel until funds run out or double up with another family, friend, or non-relatives to share a living arrangement to survive.

The term 'doubled-up' is an informal word often used to describe this type of situation but is still considered "homeless" in the McKinney-Vento Act's definition of "homeless."

In my experience, my mother, siblings, and I started off in "situational or transitional" homelessness while we were in hiding from my biological father. Eventually, I became a "couch surfer."

A couch surfer, in the context of homelessness, is a person who moves from one couch to another out of survival.

The American homeless crisis is a huge issue that I can't even begin to wrap my head around, and there are so many variables to consider from addiction, abuse, mental health, job loss, ... the list goes on.

They Were Right

Homelessness isn't something that happens overnight, even in a pandemic. There are always a series of events and choices that lead to homelessness.

Every day we make decisions that will decide how we will live a year from now or ten years from now. This is a lesson my stepdad, mother, and mentor have all tried to teach me, but I really didn't learn it until this pandemic.

Each one of them would tell me that I needed to save money and have at least six months' worth of emergency cash. My auto response was always the same, "I use my money to reinvest into my company to grow it."

My mentor had just finished hounding me, once again about my savings and boy was she right. Not even a month later, this pandemic hit, and I lost all my sources of income.

If I had not just completed one of my biggest projects, I would have not had the funds to financially survive. I would have had to let go of my team that I treasure, and I would probably be back to couch surfing.

I would be homeless. Again.

This was a huge wake up call to me. I finally learned the lesson that every decision I make will affect how I live in the future. The crazy thing is, I was not alone in how I lived my life.

In January of 2019, *Forbes* published an article reporting that 78% of workers in the United States live paycheck to paycheck and this was prior to the federal government shutdown, which affected over 800,000 federal workers.

We live in a time where our lives are on display. If you are a part of the social media craze, it's easy to put a filter on it, but that isn't real.

My harsh reality was that I wasn't saving and was merely living for the now as if it was always going to be there. I thought that I didn't have to save, just work harder. My money was spent on growing my business and having fun.

I am sure my mentor wanted to tell me, "I told you so," but instead she gave me a big hug and a spot on her couch.

I have dedicated my life to advocating for all youth with a specialty in at-risk and homeless youth. There is a huge difference between adult and youth homelessness. For the most part, youth homelessness isn't a choice they made.

Another level I don't think many people see are the individuals that live in a house but don't have a home. The person in an abusive relationship, the child whose guardian(s) are emotionally absent, etc.

To create a home, it takes so much more than four walls. With this new view I wonder how many homeless we really have.

No More False Beliefs

This "time-out" that our dear Mother Nature has put us on has caused me to look inwards. I started the first day of the pandemic scared of being homeless again, but I now know that would never happen again. I had family and friends who loved me, and for me, home was where I'm loved.

Even though I knew I would never be homeless again, metaphorically speaking. I also didn't want to be physically homeless. There's no way I'd want to go through that again.

I knew I couldn't allow this pandemic to affect my mind, so I had to shake off whatever funk it had put me in. I had to find the strength and resolve to ensure that these thoughts wouldn't consume me.

Reflective Questions:

1) Using a positive mindset, what can you do differently during and after this pandemic?

2) Have you thought about finding a mentor? Make a list of 5 people you can ask to help mentor you in life and your career.

3) Home-less can also mean "a house that is not a home," what are three things you can do to make sure your house is a home?

4) What false beliefs have you bought into that you need to change?

5) What are you doing to close the generational gap in your home?

4 STEPS TO NOT ALLOWING THE PANDEMIC TO AFFECT YOUR HOME

H.O.M.E.

STEP 3 - *Minimize Stress, Maximize Joy*

Headspace
~ From the lens of Roy

It's essential that we continually work on our emotional and mental health, no matter what life situation we find ourselves in. We have to be aware of the positions we put ourselves in and how those positions will affect us.

If I put myself in an environment that causes me to stress out, then I wouldn't be as effective in other areas of my life, like a relationship or career.

Part of keeping yourself emotionally and mentally healthy is learning to put things into perspective and surrounding yourself with individuals who have a positive outlook on life.

As a national motivational speaker, I have been able to meet so many people across the globe. Some who have remained great friends and others who I needed to separate myself from as quickly as possible.

In my travels, I met a brilliant young man by the name of Manuel "Manny" Vasquez, Jr. Manny currently works for USAA, a fortune 100 company, as a quantitative research manager and, while he is extremely successful, he wanted to use his talents and position in life to help at-risk youth, which eventually led to him working with educators and parents.

One day, I received an unsolicited call from Manny, and he told me he had heard of me through a mutual friend and colleague, Mona Aldana-Ramirez.

Mona is the Director for Equality, Diversity and Inclusive Education at San Antonio College, Texas. She has dedicated part of her career to focus on the historically marginalized and underserved populations of students within the community college system. She and I have worked extensively with The San Antonio College Men Empowerment Network (SACMEN).

During one of our conversations, I questioned how the pandemic has affected higher education.
She responded, "We find ourselves operating in a pandemic global crisis that has exposed the depth of inequities.

"But now more than ever, our students must rely on their grit and resilience to become survivors of this pandemic.

"However, we can no longer exist in systems built for students that need us the least. It is our duty to create a system of support for students that need us the most."

I believe that's why Manny and Mona connected at a young men's leadership conference at the University of Texas at Austin because he was presenting on 'Developing Long Term Goals and Dealing with Challenges as a First-Generation College Student. '

On that call, I agreed to mentor Manny and help him develop his activist career. This charismatic young man really exemplifies what it means to overcome adversity in life.

From humble beginnings in El Paso, Texas, to becoming a Ph.D. candidate studying business psychology, he has so much wisdom to offer the world.

During one of our mentoring sessions I asked Manny to share his thoughts with me on how we as a nation can minimize stress and maximize joy during a pandemic.

He said, "Wow, that's a tough one. Can I put some thought to it and email it to you in the morning?" Sure enough, the next morning his email was in my inbox.

Subject: Thoughts on Perspective, Goals, and Stress

Learning to put things in perspective is a muscle that we aren't taught to use. Being able to contextualize today's stressful and unpleasant experiences against a lifetime of happy, sad, challenging, and joyous moments helps us manage our emotions and reactions.

Without context, we are liable to get overwhelmed by the experience of failing a test, losing a loved one, missing a job opportunity, or getting into an altercation with a family member.

With context, we can learn to manage our emotions and reactions to these events.

For example, *I had a lot going on at home and got distracted this last week, so I'll ask the teacher for an opportunity to earn additional credit.*

Or, my grandfather was struggling this last year to stay with us as long as he could; I'm happy that he lived a long life close to his family and friends.

This lost job opportunity is one of 20 that I have applied to, and I've already received two additional interviews this week.

This is the first-time things got heated with my partner in a way that is not healthy; moving forward, we should learn to forgive each other and find a respectful way of disagreeing.

Helping each other nurture long-term goals is a tool we can use that promotes perspectives and hope. This begins with helping each other identify a lofty goal by asking questions like, *What is the most ambitious dream or goal that you see yourself working towards?* And, *How will you know that you've made it?*

In many ways, these long-term goals become the anchor, the point of reference for all the trials and tribulations we may experience. It also encourages forward-thinking, which highlights that we are not only where we've been but where we conceptualize where we'd like to go.

This promotes a well-rounded personal narrative consisting of; what we've experienced (the past), what we're going through (the present), and what we're working towards (the future).

As I mentioned above, and as Manny stated in his email, overcoming stress takes mental power. We must outsmart the things we're stressing about. So, what do we do when we're not in the right headspace to take on this mental battle? This is when minimizing stress and maximizing joy also becomes part of our physical health.

When we're already beaten down and can't correctly strategize how to manage our stress, we first need to focus on our mental health.

For example, going to a yoga class, catching a movie, reading a book, taking a walk (using social distancing) or even going out to grab your favorite comfort food to help clear your mind.

But there's more to it than just distracting your mind. Being well-rested, having a healthy diet, remaining positive, getting enough sleep, and staying active are just a few great ways to improve your mental health.

Of course, it may have been easier to practice some of these things outside of a pandemic; lucky for us, we have advanced technology. There are food delivery services if we can't leave the house, I've seen gyms offer their classes free online, and we can call, Facetime, or Zoom with our loved ones.

I'm not saying it's going to be easy getting out of a funk during this time, but we have to do our best and try. COVID-19 will not get the best of us.

We will continue to fight for our mental and physical health for our sake and for the people we love. Who knows, it may just take a small change to minimize our stress and maximize our joy for the day.

Show My Humanity
~ *From the lens of Consuelo*

Some may say the pandemic has paralyzed us, but for me, I refuse to give it the power over my free will and my unwavering faith.

The difference between my parents and me is they didn't show their genuine emotions, and that's something I refuse to do.

Keeping secrets and emotions held back is not healthy as they eventually get the best of you. So, if time comes to admit that I'm scared, or the state of the world gets so on top of me that I feel like crying, I will just let it happen. I don't want to just put on a brave face, I want to show my humanity with honesty and humility.

I was angry at a number of things. The pandemic caused me to lose work. I had an intern that was homesick and performing below par, and I needed his technological prowess now more than ever. I was resentful at a husband who was not with me, through no fault of his own.

He agreed to go ahead of me to Texas to prepare for our retirement. Then there were my children at home with their own issues, extended family with their problems, and just two months of payroll left. It all started to pile up, and the false beliefs began to set in.

Recalling the story of my parent's struggle and unwavering faith in the beginning of the book brought healing and gave me comfort that I, too, can make the best of this unexpected life change.

Healing can be found almost anywhere, with the right mindset. Through the lens of hope, inspiration, forgiveness, and the willingness to address a situation and not avoid it, healing is found.

Just like Roy, who has once again found himself living in a home he doesn't call his own, living with the little brother who he cared for so deeply throughout his life. He too can find healing with the right mindset, the mindset of knowing that he has a mentor that will never forsake him and a big little brother that is always guaranteed to make him laugh.

Laughing is also healing. It lowers the anxiety we feel and releases it immediately. We need more laughter as the days come, especially as the news gets bleaker. Healing is an active form of getting past our fear.

On one of the stay-at-home days, I made sure that we were doing our best to stay solvent at the same workaholic pace we had before the pandemic.

Afterward, I scolded myself. "Breathe. It's going to be okay!" I followed up with a pep talk. "Look here, you! No planes to catch, no delays, no long drives to get to clients, and more no dressing up!"

Because honestly, I'd much rather be in pajamas, and now I get to. I have day pajamas, night pajamas, and occasionally, all-day pajamas.

My family close and far away were safe; I had food and shelter. So, why so much stress? Especially since now is the time we can slow down and reflect on what Mother Nature is really trying to tell us with this pandemic.

Still, Roy and I are the breadwinners of our home, so we both stress a bit. Many people take pride that they work best under pressure, and I am one of them, which has also caused me not to be healthy, overwhelm myself, and get upset. I am still learning to minimize my stress and maximize my joy, for we are so blessed.

It Looks Like Pee

In the earlier chapter, I mentioned listing five things you were grateful for, and it made me think of how many things I am grateful for; among them are my family, Roy, Greg, and our employees. Even if we are without some things, I know others are struggling more, and our prayers go out to them.

We have an opportunity, due to the pandemic, to slow down, be grateful and use other talents we possess. It's been incredible connecting with many of my friends during this time.

I am amused to see my grandchildren learning virtually. One cute story involves my grandson Dorian (who was born on my birthday) learning about Science. (Alicia, my daughter, shared it with me via text.)

"Mom, I am sending you a funny video of your grandson. We were creating sugar water for hummingbirds. 1-part sugar meant 4 parts water. Hence, 1 cup of sugar needed to be diluted in 4 cups of water.

As I watched the video, the funny part was when he asked what have you learned? He quickly answered, it looks like pee! I am keeping the video and waiting until he's old enough to date. Then I'm going to bring it out — mwahahaha (Evil grandma laugh).

Before the pandemic, my excuse was that I was traveling or training all day. But now, I have more time to stop, think, and reflect on what is truly important in life: the people you love.

Admittedly, I have ADD/ADHD, and am a workaholic due to my upbringing, which is why I work so hard.

Dirty Little Fingers

When I was nine years old, I went downtown with my mother. It was April, and all the store windows were beautifully decorated in the Easter Bunny tradition.

I was so taken by the beautiful dresses and how they hung on hangers rather than boxes like in the thrift stores my mother and I would go to. Then I saw the Big Giant Rabbit and the basket with Eggs. It was stunning, so I put my little hands on the glass to see better.

Shortly after, a woman came out and shouted at my mother. "You know there is nothing in this store you can afford, so why do you let your child put her dirty little fingers on the window?!"

I cast my eyes down as my mother apologized and offered to clean the window. If you will give me something to clean it with," she began, "I will be more than happy to do it."

The woman called a gentleman out from the back room to give my mother a rag. He seemed embarrassed that my mother was scolded and offered to do it himself, but the woman protested.

"She will clean it; it was her grubby daughter who dirtied the window." My mother scrubbed the window as the lady at the store stared her down. As my mother gave the rag back and apologized, we left.

When we got out of sight of the woman, my mother grabbed my hand, bent down enough for me to feel her breath on my face, and said, "You know that we can't afford any of those things, so why did you do that?"

She continued with words of wisdom that would define my work ethic and moral compass, "I believe that one day, with God's will and your learning—since you love school—you will go into that store and never have to apologize. But most importantly, no matter how far you get in life, never disrespect or minimize people for everyone has value."

This story has stayed with me and what still haunts me is that people can be so cruel and hurtful to one another. Little did I know this was about economic class.

With the pandemic, we will face far more economic divides but kindness, compassion, patience, and understanding knows no class; it all comes from the heart.

It's Been So Long
~ *From the lens of Roy*

*O**ur humanity is found*** in the joy we bring to others, so bring so much joy into someone's life, that they can't help but smile or laugh. It's in those moments that everything fades away—all the fear, pain, and hardship—even if it's only for a brief moment.

Humor will minimize stress and maximize joy; it is the medicine to our souls because it is hope.

Ask yourself, who can I bring hope to today? Is it your significant other? Your children or grandchildren? Your family, friends, or neighbors? These little gestures will keep our humanity intact, and this will keep our love strong enough to get through anything.

During this "time-out," you would think we would have an excess amount of time, but it's been quite the opposite. My team and I have been working unconventional hours brainstorming, creating, researching, and projecting. We've been doing everything we could to ensure our company, IMPACTtruth, survived and thrived through these unprecedented events.

Staying with my mentor, I watched her team and her work just as hard. Together we kept each other productive and accountable. Encouraging each other to be innovative and not lose hope. It seemed as though we were moving at a million miles an hour.

Deciding which tasks are more important was taxing, emotionally challenging, and quarantined didn't help clear the fog.

I can no longer move my workspace to the local coffee shop if I'm unable to focus in the house, or in this case, my mentor's condo. So how am I relieving the stress of being confined when there are so many things to be done? This is where the decision making comes into play.

Often, we find ourselves feeling guilty for not doing specific tasks that we should be doing or putting them off for 'tomorrow.' For example, Ray took a couple of hours to himself the other day and practiced social distancing when he went for a hike. He invited Greg; however, when Greg saw one of Ray's previous hikes on video, he declined and quickly went back to slamming doors in the kitchen. There were no hundred-foot drops to be found in there!

Because my little brother decided to go hiking instead of working in the condo with us, should he feel guilty? No, of course not! Was it more important? Maybe to him, because being stuck in a 1,500 square foot condo with Six other people can take a toll on you mentally, besides I'd much rather have a mentally healthy Ray working by my side.

Now, decision making isn't always as easy as choosing to go for a hike to clear our mind or continuing to work while our brains are fried. It may make you feel guilty for the parents out there if you choose to watch a movie over doing the dishes right after dinner or folding the laundry, but please know it's okay.

One of my team members mentioned that she felt sorry for not putting in enough hours because, as a single mother, she is working around the clock to take care of her daughter. As a company, we believe in family-first and have allowed her to work whenever she could.

During this time, you might even feel obligated to be productive while staying at home because you just want to be able to say you did something that day. It is okay to take a healthy break. You will be more productive when you are in the right mindset.

I would offer this warning out of my personal experience. Always keep a healthy work-life balance. It is easy to develop unhealthy habits that can negatively affect you.

Once, I was burning the candle at both ends, on a national tour. I woke up in my hotel in Chicago and had temporarily lost my eyesight. My doctor related it to my stress levels.

However, it's one thing to take a "healthy break" and another to use it as an excuse for laziness, but only you will know the difference.

We all have the same 24 hours. We can't slow down or speed up time, and we can only do what we think is best in those hours.

World Case Scenario

During the pandemic, it will require us to make decisions we wouldn't be making otherwise. Decisions like, which subscriptions to keep, whether to freeze a gym membership, whether or not to use Uber Eats, ...

The examples listed are on the lighter side, and I can't give specific recommendations as I am unfamiliar with your financial situation. I understand that some really tough decisions are being made that could be the difference between your family eating or going hungry, and I don't make light of that. Only you know what's best for your family.

As a business owner, I wanted to save every penny to keep my team employed as long as possible. I canceled every company and personal subscription that I could, except for Netflix.

Netflix allowed me to binge-watch a show when I needed to break away mentally. Did you watch Tiger King?! Joe Exotic for President! Who's with me? (Okay, maybe I've been in quarantine too long.) Back to my point, it's important to be aware of our decision-making process because we don't want to fall into the trap of emotional decision making.

Emotional decision making can be a dangerous place to be because often, regret is tied to it. Think about the last time you made a decision with your emotions, maybe it was something you bought and returned two days later, or perhaps you sent a text message you wished you could take back.

Emotional decision making happens all the time, and most of the time, they aren't very detrimental. However, plenty of decisions can be. If we trace the lines of our choices, who is affected?

Let's look at a hypothetical scenario.

> Chris, his partner Taylor, and their two children Jason and Maria were all in quarantine together.
>
> **Day 1:** Everything seemed normal. Chris and Taylor did their usual routine — Chris made breakfast for the family, the kids played in the room, and Taylor worked at home off the computer.
>
> **Day 2:** Similar to day one other than a few more dirty dishes in the sink, laundry to do, and noise from the restless children running around. Taylor took her makeshift office from the living room to the bedroom for a little more peace and quiet.

Day 3: Chris served cereal because the dishes were dirty, and he started to feel unappreciated and wondered why he was the only one cooking. The kids began fighting with each other and Taylor was frustrated with everyone because they couldn't understand that she was the only breadwinner in the house.

Day 4: Now the emotional decision making takes place.

Chris yells at Taylor, "You don't even help around the house."

Taylor yells back, "Help? I am the only one bringing in money to support this family."

(In the other room the kids are fighting too. Jason is yelling at his sister Maria, which makes her cry.)

Chris yells, "screw this" and storms out of the house.

Taylor, who is now left carrying the whole load, has to cook, clean, watch the kids and work to bring in money.

Chris comes back a little tipsy because he went to a friend's house who was also dealing with being cooped up.

Worst case scenario: Several days later, Chris and his daughter begin to show symptoms of the virus.

I know this scenario is extreme but is it that farfetched? Each adult made a series of decisions based on their emotions, and with just a little communication, the situation could have been avoided. The outcome was a family that suffered emotionally and physically.

My Eyes Welled Up

In a real-life scenario, I wonder how it happened for my parents. A series of emotional decisions led them down a path and would eventually lead to me being homeless at the age of 14.

Suddenly this "hypothetical example" becomes a little more real, especially for kids like me.

According to a 2019 online news article entitled; "10 Facts about Homelessness in America by U.S. News and World Report," an estimated 700,000 youth under age 18 without a parent or guardian experience homelessness each year, according to the National Law Center on Homelessness and Poverty. Often they are in their situation as a result of parental mental health issues, parental abuse or neglect, severe family conflict, or being forced to leave home after sharing that they are pregnant or identify as LGBTQ."

I know we all have to make decisions right now and some will be harder than others and as a past homeless kid, I beg you, please make healthy choices.

Let your children or family walk away from quarantine with fun and beautiful memories. You have the power to create a positive home environment through conscious decision making.

Emotional decision making is sometimes the easiest choice, but more often than not, it's not the best. When writing this book, this section actually became a trigger for me and my eyes welled up and I questioned, *how many more "little Roys" must suffer?*

We're all spending time in the house, staying busy, but are we spending quality time with each other? I jumped on a call with my team to discuss business, but we all began sharing our quarantine stories.

Reggie, my Operations Manager, shared that she had joined her boyfriend's family for dinner. As the six of them sat together at the table, passing food around, she looked over and noticed her boyfriend's little brother was crying.

She said, "I didn't know what to do, so I just watched as his dad got up to comfort him and asked, 'is everything okay'?

Then his little brother looked up and said 'I'm just happy, it's really nice that we're having dinner together. It's been so long."

She continued, "I was so confused, aren't they quarantined together? They're with each other all the time!"
It was an eye-opener to hear her story. How can the people we spend all day next to, feel a distance between us still? In my case, Mrs. Kickbusch, her daughters, Greg, Ray, and I are all cooped up, working away.

Work has been our top priority, the first task on our list of things to do, and although there is a sense of urgency to create new content during this time, it's not more important than staying mentally healthy and connecting with each other.

A healthy decision would be for me to step away from this computer and see if anyone wants to play a boardgame with me. I encourage you to do the same. Take a pause from this book and go make a memory!

Reflective Questions:

1) What wisdom did you gain from Mrs. Kickbusch 'mother's story?

2) Where do you find your healing and laughter?

3) What five actions will you take as a result of the pandemic towards strengthening your bond and ties with family, friends, and colleagues?

4) What will you do this week to take time for yourself? (It's always okay to make time for yourself.)

5) What is your process for decision making? How can preventing emotional decisions strengthen your family?

The follow are ideas you can use as tools during these strange times.

- Ask the kids at home what they would love to do. Even if they come up with some absurd ideas, humor them at this time and allow them to express their enthusiasm and creativity. Remember kids have emotions too.

- Challenge yourself to organize some Karaoke or dress up for a date in the next room with your significant other.

- Play Virtual Monopoly or another game online that can connect you to your family and friends. (We have been playing bingo with small wagers, really small wagers (beans), so don't turn us into the Vegas Gaming Commission!) Buenas!

- As a family, create an "I am grateful for" list and name five things you are grateful for. Afterwards, ask each person to share and discuss their lists.

- Read spiritual books that'll help you through this trying time.

- Get in the kitchen, create a new family recipe or teach an old one!

- Have a drawing contest.

- Make a memory book.

- Learn the lyrics to songs from your child's favorite Disney movie.

- Go wild, color your hair — no one will see it!

- Make a crazy, "I survived the pandemic" ugly shirt.

- Give your kids a 'timeout from parents 'card.

- Give yourself an at-home spa day.

- Make those memories, they are a lifetime gift!

- Learn to play your kids favorite video game.

- Write and mail handwritten letters to friends and family!

- As a family, binge-watch a show on Netflix or YouTube. I suggest Psych or Threes Company.

- Get creative and create your own boardgame.

The options are limitless!!!

H.O.M.E.

STEP 4 - *Educate & Empower*

Pup vs. the Big Dog! Ruff-ruff.
~ From the lens of Consuelo

As promised, I was going to tell you a story about the youngest member of my team, Ray, who I lovingly refer to as Pup.

Pup is a recent college graduate, who signed up for a year internship to learn about life lessons and business. He even agreed to live in my living room to cut down on cost.

His goal is to save $30,000, which will eventually go towards his dream of owning a coffee shop, which will feature many of Greg's sandwiches that he fed us during this pandemic.

In return, he would travel with me, have all his expenses paid, and learn as much as he could from every opportunity that my small company could provide.

Pup is talented; however, I knew that, unlike Roy, he was given far more comforts. He was also the baby of his family and stayed with his mother, who lived the middle-class life. So why was he not performing?

It would be easy for someone in my generation to write him off as a "mommas' boy" who has lived a suburban life with pretty much everything handed to him, including a paid-for college degree.

I was frustrated because this kid has so much talent and wasn't using any of it. Pup has aspirations of being wealthy and being his own boss. However, his lack of motivation and performance was starting to, to put it bluntly, piss me off.

I needed all hands-on deck to keep this company alive, not slacking and excuses. I was continuously agitated seeing him tap away on his smartphone, and to me, it wasn't a particularly 'smart 'way to use your time. I wanted him to use his marketing degree and his expertise in social media to help us emerge from this pandemic.

Things got to a boiling point. When we sat down, the big dog and the pup had to have a heart to heart, and Pup admitted that he really wanted to go home, but he knew he couldn't because of COVID-19.

He admitted he was struggling with the feeling of "fight or flight." He wanted to stay because it was an opportunity to learn and make money that could go towards his dream, but he felt like he didn't have a home. He felt homeless.

I tried to help him understand that he was loved and welcomed in our home, and I understood what he was feeling. However, as a mentor, I needed to push him and be tough.

I questioned, "What is your plan B, and how much will that cost you?" Then I questioned some more, "Are you pleased with your work ethic? Would you hire you? Put yourself in my shoes."

It's not easy to help a young man develop and mature as a professional, and frankly speaking, many CEOs wouldn't even bother to invest the time. I believe this is where my generation misses the point. We have to invest in the next generation because if we don't, then we can't complain about their leadership style — the blame would fall solely on us.

My view on courageous leadership has always been service before profit because God knows this young man has an appetite and isn't cheap, but I will always put food on his plate. The one area I can't help him with is his illness for the ladies. I am going to need therapy for that one once his internship is over!

Pup's lens and my lens are quite different, but we aren't competing, we are working towards understanding each other. The complexity of leadership is trying to define the line between toughness and compassion. Once that line is defined, it's even more difficult not to cross. There are a number of ways to stay cooperative, and not minimizing or dismissing each other's experiences. Empathy and understanding are the best way for this.

So, in this instance, the big dog needed to remove the claws, and I needed to make it a point to understand Pup as best as possible. I knew his parents were in quarantine back in Texas, and he had nowhere to go at this time.

The solution was a compromise. He would try harder and I, although still stern, would remind him that I loved him, and would be clearer whenever I was dissatisfied with his performance.

Pup is young, and if we're transparent, we all have probably let someone down in our journey in the short term. However, transparency is likely to bring long term benefits.

Your children or whomever you are—shall I lovingly say—stuck with, will challenge you, and it's not all about winning. Even if you are right, there is no need to turn it into a verbal contest.

I know I am tough, and some may even think that I'm mean, but I am not helping Pup by being an enabler. I wish nothing more than for him to realize his dream.

However, his dreams can only be realized if they are built on a foundation of integrity, strong work ethic, helping others, and the push to be self-driven and knowledgeable. I will always be there to give him my guidance, my direction, and most importantly, my endless love.

The greatest gift Pup has given me was helping me to "put myself in his shoes." This remarkable young man was sleeping on my sofa, depressed and worried about his parents, his siblings, and his friends with whom he has very strong bonds. (It's a generational thing.)

The reality is I have at least two of my five children that I see every day, and they have their rooms and me to take care of them. I need to maintain empathy and compassion. I need to find balance when lines are blurred. I believe everyone from my generation (Boomer) needs to ponder these things too.

My generation, while it struggles and even mocks the millennials/GenZ, can accept that the young ones know how to instinctively find what needs to be done using technology.

These newer generations do it quickly and have no problem jumping into a video game as professional development. Now is their era, and their virtual world is the world we boomers must catch up on. They are technology's natives, and we are the confused tourists in need of learning and respecting their customs.

Coffee and a Hallelujah

The next morning, I had hoped Pup had turned his attitude and emotions around. Sure enough—Hallelujah! —he came into my bedroom/office with a fresh cup of coffee.

We sat down like we usually do and listened to the news. Right in front of us were warnings about Cabin Fever. Pup lit up and turned around pointing at himself whenever the symptoms were mentioned, points like:

- Radical Mood Swings
- Resentment of People, Especially Folks with Authority
- Feelings of Isolation
- Irrational Behavior

"That's me!" he said.

"No Pup," I responded. "That's your generation."

We both laughed.

I continued, "Are you going to apologize? Because change cannot happen until you accept your role."

While there is no medical proof of "Cabin Fever" we can agree it does exist and many of us are knee deep in it. I am happy to note that Pup did the noble thing and apologized. I told you he's a great kid.

If you are at home and struggling with the close-quarters you find yourself in due to the COVID-19, it is crucial that you pay attention to your emotions.

Maybe mood swings are getting the best of you, or perhaps you are getting Cabin Fever as you are indoors and closer to people than you would otherwise be.

Another source on Cabin Fever describes the feeling that comes with being isolated in a particular place (like a building, room, house, etc.) for some time.

Usually, this feeling coincides with extreme isolation, much like some of us are experiencing now. Another newscast (Okay I think we are watching too much TV.) listed these points on the screen for us to ask ourselves if it's what we may be feeling:

- Stressed or restless
- A sense of sadness or depression

- Weight loss or weight gain
- Having trouble concentrating or the inability to cope with our stress

(A trained mental health professional would be the one to make a diagnosis. Also, not everyone may feel this way, and more power to you if you've mentally handled it well so far. But to those who haven't been, again, it's okay to reach out and ask for help.)

The Wellness Program

In preparation for this book, we looked at the many films made during my two decades of motivational speaking, and frankly, I hadn't watched most of them.

Although I have been on stage with numerous celebrities and spoken in front of large crowds, I am mostly shy and reserved. I have never written my keynotes for I search my heart, trust the good Lord to guide me, and include the many experiences I have witnessed about hope and transformation.

In preparation for my keynotes and workshops, I do read countless books, for I too need healing, motivation, and am a life learner. There is no greater story to tell than your own. It serves as a double dose of Hope.

It reminds you how far you have come and inspires others to stretch themselves and realize that it is possible to Dream Big. With the pandemic over our heads and weighing heavy in our hearts, we can't help but wonder what will happen to our jobs and our lives.

I have the following thought to offer you. "Although your job may have ended, your talents are still with you. The opportunity lies with how you use them now."

For example, Roy and I could have given up, realizing we could not travel anywhere, and would it even be proper to "sell" our message. However, we needed to stay employed. Roy and I thought foremost, what do people need more of, that we can serve using our talents, our stories, and love for humanity. Among the many "gifts" we decided to give were free podcasts and webinars, food baskets, donations, and bringing other well-known speakers to join our cause to help and inspire our fellow mankind not to give up.

This book is among the many ideas we chose to do in just two weeks, and if you see the pictures, you will know we weren't winning any beauty contests, so go ahead and laugh with us or at us.

What kept us going was our family, our employees, and you. A huge thank you for giving us your support by downloading our Labor of Love. Greg, our chef in residence and Pup, the kid that was now performing, accompanied us through this journey. I know Greg's delicious food has put about ten more pounds on this already robust figure of mine.

It is incredible to watch Pup explode with ideas, creativity, and innovation. Could it be because I promised he would get to go home and connect with one of his… Mmm… I'll stop there. It's all part of his wellness program.

Dig Myself Out of a Hole

If you are someone who has lost their job, as challenging as it may seem, take this experience one step at a time and don't lose faith. Stay away from those False Beliefs and know that it is okay to be vulnerable and seek help.

I recall a painful time in my life when I thought I was doing well. I had worked hard to get myself through school, had a nice, beautiful home, and a fancy car. I was leading men in the military and raising three daughters. It felt like I made it.

Well, while some would say my life looked like the American Dream, the truth was it was becoming a nightmare. My marriage had fallen apart, the divorce got ugly, and in a matter of a few months, I became a single mom with three girls to raise and bills mounting by the day.

Life didn't stop for me, and my military career didn't slow down a bit. I was still expected to do my seven-mile run at 0600 hours AM. I now had to leave my children's clothes and meals on the table, and rush to work.

During the day, I prepared lesson plans for my military officers, ran back home to deal with homework, and in the evenings, I would teach in a maximum security prison as an adjunct professor to make ends meet.

When I asked for help, a dear friend whom I had hired some time ago said, "You were there for me, and now I will be there for you. I will work for free and stay with your children while you get back on your feet."

Although it was a while later, I paid her back, for what she gave me was a chance to leverage my talents and dig myself out of a hole. My children paid that price with me, a lesson I don't wish on anyone.

I remember we did a lot of window shopping, but we walked together on weekends, and enjoyed a Happy Meal because we were happy to be together. I feel so blessed to share with you that my kids were grateful, even in our toughest times.

They didn't complain about wearing my clothes to school the next year, eating quick microwavable meals, how the house had no furniture for a while, or that the car I drove now had a hole in the muffler, so the whole neighborhood knew when I was coming home.

All they cared about was the love I had for them, and I wasn't going to let anyone take them away from me. The truth is the way kids spell love is T.I.M.E.

The Army never did find out about my woes, for you have to be tough to continue to lead. The two or three people I trusted never said a word, and instead stood by me and kept me sane.

As a person that believes strongly in Education and Empowerment, I use this story in my training as we should not allow the negativity from other people to destroy our dreams.

We have the power to Dream Big and change our lives. Our vision has no limits, and with hard work, perhaps now more than ever, we will be able to use our talents differently and leverage through collaboration and community.

Back to the Basics
~ From the lens of Roy

***C**hange is constant,* and with change can come growth. Not too long before COVID-19, the changes in my life were minor. Every now and then I would have to switch flights last minute, and sometimes I was more consciously choosing my foods for a healthier lifestyle. If there were any major changes, they were planned. However, even planned changes can have unplanned results.

Nothing could have prepared us for this. In a matter of two weeks, we saw news channels advising us not to worry, even though several states were on lockdown.

People were losing their jobs, income, and most tragically, some were losing their life. Unlike the many other instances of where we've had to adjust, this pandemic is far more alarming because of the unknown — even the experts aren't sure of exactly what to do with this new beast.

As Mrs. Kickbusch mentioned above, although some of us have lost our jobs, let us not forget what matters most and that is family. Embrace change, for it is constant and it is here.

I think I speak for a majority of people when I say that little things we took for granted like going to the grocery store, having a date night, or simply visiting a family member would become so complex. Our lives have done a complete 180.

I went from traveling up to 25 days every month to staying in one confined area for a prolonged period, with no end in sight. I acknowledge my negative emotions, but just as quickly as I feel myself getting frustrated, I let them go.

We have to take positive action despite feeling pessimistic. We can't let negative emotions like fear, panic, and distrust take over our humanity. This pandemic will not stop us from growing. Our growth will be a valuable act of resistance.

When faced with adversity, neither IMPACTtruth, Inc. nor Educational Achievement Services, Inc. thought about giving up.

Of course, we were shocked, worried, and confused, but instead of throwing in the towel, Mrs. Kickbusch and I decided to brainstorm, create, and thrive as best we could. COVID-19 wasn't about to stop us from progressing as leaders; we needed to embrace change and grow with it.

As odd as it may sound, being pushed into the virtual world has been a blessing for my company. We're now seriously exploring how to hold virtual meetings and seminars, which will allow people from across the globe to hear our messages of love, unity, and togetherness.

During the pandemic I hired a new member to my team, Jose Torres, a young man who approached me, after one of my lectures and asked if he could make a documentary of my family's story. It was the perfect timing because we need someone with his skills. He hit the ground running with so many ideas for a short documentary and has been working on podcasts as an avenue for reaching new audiences.

We can't control what's happening, but we can control our response.

We can choose to look at the positives of the current state of our world. For example, look around, our planet is healing because there are fewer cars on the street and less pollution. Even the canals in Venice, Italy have cleared, and dolphins and swans have moved back in.

Now it's time to allow our families to heal, we can take our cue from Mother Nature. Let us remove the pollution from our lives and allow our families to get back to the basics, love, faith and hope.

4 STEPS TO NOT ALLOWING THE PANDEMIC TO AFFECT YOUR HOME

Reflective Questions

1) Find clarity and ask yourself questions: What am I able to control? What must I sacrifice?

2) What are your talents, and how will you now use them differently?

3) Has this pandemic pushed you to re-think about how happy and content you were with your job? If it has, will you make the change?

4) Will you now invest in yourself by taking advantage of the new virtual opportunities available?

5) If your job is one of those that was not lost yet disrupted, what will you do differently upon your return?

Final Thoughts

Thank you so much for reading our short guide to overcoming a pandemic, emotionally and mentally. We hope that you found this book useful and inspiring to read it as we did to write it.

We wrote it with the hope to help families get through this tough time.

No matter what life throws at us, even if it is as confusing and challenging as a pandemic, it is crucial we treat everything as a chance to self-reflect, learn, and grow to become stronger human beings.

As with everything else, this will pass. Life is full of hardships and unwelcome surprises, but it's how we respond to them.

Always remember what really matters, family, health, faith, hope, and love.

Once again, thank you to all those on the front line. More so, our hearts go out to those who have lost love ones. Our prayers are with you.

With all our love and respect,

~ Roy and Consuelo

Other Books by These Authors

Journey to the Future
Author: RET. LTC Consuelo Castillo Kickbusch

www.EASLeadership.com

Synopsis:

Consuelo's first book, *Journey to the Future*, is a primer for middle and high school-aged children to develop personal goals and a framework for early leadership development. It encourages and tutors them to create life goals and plan for the future. *Journey to the Future* asks its readers to look within themselves and reflect, thus helping them learn and improve.

Homeless by Choice: A Memoir of Love, Hate, and Forgiveness
Author: Roy Juarez, Jr.

www.IMPACTtruth.com

Synopsis:

This riveting memoir journeys through Roy's decision to live homeless once again, but this time, Homeless by Choice, with a mission to inspire youth to never give up on life, their dreams and understand the power of higher education. This journey would lead him to uncover the hidden issues that plague America's youth. Surprised by what he finds, Roy is forced to face his own childhood and the demons that have haunted him for years. Just because you have a house doesn't mean you have a home.

About the Authors

RET. LTC Consuelo Castillo Kickbusch

The values **Consuelo Castillo Kickbusch** learned as a child were reinforced throughout her career in the United States Army.

After graduating from Hardin Simmons University, Consuelo entered the U.S. Army as an officer and served for two decades. During that time, she broke barriers and set records in the military where she became the highest-ranking Hispanic woman in the Combat Support Field of the U.S. Army.

When the opportunity arose to assume a command post, Consuelo shocked the military by deciding to retire. She chose to honor her mother's dying wish – for her to return to her roots and become a community leader. In 1996, Consuelo Castillo Kickbusch founded the human development company, Educational

Achievement Services, Inc. (EAS, Inc.), to fulfill her mission of preparing tomorrow's leaders.

Consuelo Castillo Kickbusch currently shares her story with people of all ages and creeds. She is doing exactly what she preaches – living a legacy. Her dedication to inspiring the youth of America has led Consuelo to work with over one million children and their parents across the United States.

Consuelo's clients include: Wal-Mart, State Farm Insurance, Ford Motor Company, General Motors Corporation, Costco, Sodexo, Dell, Boeing, Nordstrom, Lockheed-Martin, the National Football League, Avon, IBM, Verizon, U.S. Postal Service, U.S Drug Enforcement Agency, Department of Education, NASA-Ames Research, and many others.

Consuelo Castillo Kickbusch is the proud mother of five daughters, the proud grandmother of four, and currently resides in Las Vegas with her husband, David.

Stay Connected:

Website: www.EASLeadership.com
Instagram: www.instagram.com/eas_leadership
Twitter: www.twitter.com/ConsueloEAS
Facebook:
www.facebook.com/consuelo.c.kickbusch

4 STEPS TO NOT ALLOWING THE PANDEMIC TO AFFECT YOUR HOME

Roy Juarez, Jr.

Roy Juarez Jr. founded IMPACTtruth, Inc.—a human development company—in 2005 with a dream to reunite families and inspire youth to never give up.

Juarez's story began on the Southside of San Antonio, Texas, where he faced dangerous situations and obstacles that could have turned him into a negative statistic.

At the age of fourteen, Juarez—due to domestic violence—became a high school drop-out and one of the hundreds of homeless youth on the streets of San Antonio. With only a duffle bag of personal items that he called home; Juarez moved from house to house to survive.

Thanks to the ministers, Juarez returned to high school as a third-year freshman, graduating in 2000. He then went on to study Business Administration at Hardin-Simmons University and graduated in 2009.

Juarez fought the battle to leave the streets only to return to them as an activist after finishing college. Juarez has shared his message with over a million students, parents, educators, and service providers in every state in the United States and abroad through his work.

In 2018, Juarez published his highly anticipated book, *Homeless by Choice: A Memoir of Love, Hate, and Forgiveness.* This riveting memoir journeys through Roy's decision to live homeless once again, but this time, Homeless by Choice. His mission was to inspire youth to never give up on life, their dreams, and for them to understand the power of higher education.

During the pandemic, Juarez used his time to dive deeper into his work and created tools to expand his reach and share his message of hope.

He co-authored his second book, this book. Produced a documentary entitled ROY, published a children's book entitled The Adventures of James and Roy, expanded his company into a speakers bureau, opened

IMPACT Publishing, Inc, and published his 1st client's book entitled, Embracing Me – A Memoir by actor and speaker April Hernandez Castillo.

Juarez has partnered with national organizations and companies such as the U.S. ARMY, Ford Motor Company Fund, and the United States Hispanic Leadership Institute to inspire thousands of individuals across the United States and abroad. His work has garnered national media attention on outlets such as CNN, Chicken Soup for the Soul, and many local and online publications.

Stay Connected

Website: www.RoyJuarezJr.com
LinkedIn: www.LinkedIn.com/in/RoyJuarezJr
Facebook: www.Facebook.com/RoyJuarezJr
Instagram: www.Instagram.com/RoyJuarezJr
Twitter: www.Twitter.com/RoyJuarezJr
YouTube: www.YouTube.com/RoyJuarezJr

4 STEPS TO NOT ALLOWING THE PANDEMIC TO AFFECT YOUR HOME

www.ingramcontent.com/pod-product-compliance
Lightning Source LLC
Chambersburg PA
CBHW071350080526
44587CB00017B/3044